W9-BVA-007

A PRAYER BOOK

FOR THE TWENTY-FIRST CENTURY

Morehouse Publishing, P.O. Box 1321, Harrisburg, PA 17105

Morehouse Publishing is a member of the Continuum International Publishing Group.

Cover art courtesy of Bob Rowan, Progressive Image/Corbis. All rights reserved

Cover design by Laurie Klein Westhafer

Library of Congress Cataloging-in-Publication Data

McQuiston, John.

A prayer book for the 21st century / by John McQuiston II.
    p. cm.
Includes bibliographical references.
ISBN 0-8192-1974-6
1. Prayers. I. Title: Prayer book for the twenty-first century.
II. Title.
BV260.M36 2004
242^1.803--dc21

                                        2003011435

Printed in the United States of America

03 04 05 06 07 08 10 9 8 7 6 5 4 3 2 1

In our longing for a god, we try again and again to set up a greater, a more genuine and more just image, which is intended to be more glorious than the last and only proves the more unsatisfactory. . . . The images topple, but the voice is never silenced. . . . The voice speaks in the guise of everything that happens. . . . It does not matter what you call it. All that matters is that you hear it.

—MARTIN BUBER[1]

We do not know whether we shall succeed in once more expressing the spiritual form of our future communities in the old religious language.

—WERNER HEISENBERG[2]

God is the beyond in our midst.

—DIETRICH BONHOEFFER[3]

CONTENTS

ACKNOWLEDGMENTS

My first and greatest thank you is to my family. Throughout my life they have been, and are, the paramount expressions of the Sacred Presence for me.

Thanks to Phyllis Tickle, author, brilliant commentator on contemporary developments in religion, and friend. From the beginning of our friendship, she assumed that I was better than I really am, and by that generous and misguided view, she continually challenges me to attempt to live up to her opinion.

Debra Farrington provided all that anyone could ask of an editor: faith in the concept, and valuable shaping of the manuscript.

FOREWORD

How we think about God, the language we use for prayer, and what we think prayer is about are very closely connected. Thus, when I was invited to write a foreword for this book by John McQuiston and told that its subject is "prayers to a panentheistic God," I was immediately interested.

Panentheism—a way of thinking about God known in Christianity and in most religions—has been immensely important in my own life. And though I grew up Christian, I became aware of panentheism only in my adulthood. After the last vestiges of my childhood way of thinking about God had fallen away, panentheism made it possible for me to recover a robust sense of the reality of God and a deepening life of prayer. It not only removed what had become the primary intellectual stumbling block to taking God seriously, but it also transformed my understanding and practice of prayer. God and prayer were resurrected together.

Panentheism, a term not always recognized by readers but which I'll explain very shortly, is one of two primary concepts of God in Christianity, and in perhaps all religions. The other is commonly called "supernatural theism." As root images or basic models for imagining God and the God-world relationship, each has quite different answers to these questions:

- To what does the word "God" refer? What do we have in mind when we use this word? What are we thinking of?
- "Where" is God in relation to the universe? "Out there"? "Right here"? Or?
- And what is God's relationship to the world? Does God intervene?
- Or does God relate to the world in a different manner?

The differences between these two concepts of God are central to this book as well as religiously important in our time.

Of these two concepts, supernatural theism is

more familiar. Most of us grew up with it. For it, the word "God" refers to a person-like being "up there" or "out there." A long time ago, this being created the universe as a reality separate from God. Thus, "where" is God in relation to the universe? The God of supernatural theism is "beyond," "out there," and not "here." How does this person-like being relate to the universe? Through intervention from "out there": it is the only way a "separate" God can relate to the world.

The God of supernatural theism is thus an interventionist. Within this framework, the spectacular events reported in the Bible are understood as God's interventions in the past. Most people who think of God this way affirm that God continues to intervene to this day, even if not as spectacularly as in biblical times.

This is the basic idea of God that formed in my mind during childhood. It was the result of the language for God that I heard and learned in church. The Bible (and the Christian tradition as a whole) is rich with the language of supernatural theism. By "the language of supernatural theism," I simply mean language that personifies God by speaking of God as if God were a person, a being separate from other beings.

The opening words of the best-known Christian prayer use such language: "Our Father who art in heaven." So also, addressing God as king, lord, shepherd, and so forth, easily suggests that God is a person, just as we are persons, even though with utterly superlative qualities.

Such personification is the natural language of worship, devotion, and prayer. There is nothing wrong with it, so long as it is not literalized or semi-literalized. But when it is, whether in harder or softer forms, it does create problems. "Hard" literalization of this language is relatively uncommon; though the Bible speaks of God as having hands, eyes, ears, mouth, and so forth, few people think that God really does have such features. But softer literalization of this language is quite common: not that God has hands, and so forth, but that God nevertheless is a person-like being.

This is what happened to me by the end of

childhood. Gradually and quite unconsciously, the combined effect of the language of supernatural theism generated the notion that the word "God" really does refer to a person-like being "out there." *This* is what the word "God" meant. And it shaped my understanding of prayer. So long as this understanding of God remained intact, the meaning of prayer was obvious. Prayer was about talking to this person-like being, confessing my sins, asking for forgiveness, blessing my family and friends, and asking for God to intervene. Prayer made perfect sense.   My experience is typical, I think. Supernatural theism is the most common understanding of the word "God" in our culture. It is what theologian Kenneth Leech calls "conventional western theism." It is widely held by "believers" and "unbelievers" alike. The former believe there is such a person-like being; the latter do not. But both are believing or rejecting *the same concept of God.*

I find this among my university students. When one of them says to me, "I don't really believe in God," I always say, "Tell me about the God you don't believe in." Invariably, it is the God of supernatural theism. And most of them are unaware that there is another concept of God, another way of thinking about God.

So it was for me. As my teens and twenties unrolled, the God of supernatural theism became less and less persuasive, and prayer began to make less and less sense. I had difficulty imagining a being "out there" beyond the universe. I thus had trouble imagining that anybody was listening to my prayers.

I also had trouble believing that God sometimes intervened. The problem, then and now, was the non-interventions: If God sometimes intervenes, how does one account for the non-interventions? If God could have intervened to stop the Holocaust, but chose not to—what kind of sense does that make? The question arises with less public events as well. Does it make sense that God intervenes to heal some people or to rescue some from accidents but not others?

Because of my concept of God, formed to a large extent by the language of supernatural theism, I became a practical atheist, and prayer became highly problematic. Yet I struggled to believe in such a God, for it was the only concept of God I knew. I was not successful. Supernatural theism had become the primary intellectual obstacle in my life with God.

Panentheism removed this obstacle and revivified my life with God. As a way of thinking about God, it sees all of these matters quite differently. As John McQuiston points out in his introduction to this book, the Greek roots of the word mean "everything (*pan*) is in (*en*) God (*theos*)." The middle syllable *en* has a double meaning: everything in God, and God in everything.

To cite the most concise biblical expression of panentheism, God is "the one in whom we live and move and have our being" (Acts 17:28). Notice how the language works: Where are we in relation to God? We live in God, we move in God, we have our being in God. God is not somewhere else, but "right here," all around us. God is the encompassing Spirit in whom everything that is, is.

Thus panentheism does not think of God as "a being." To clarify, it does not think of God as a being separate from other beings, not as another being in addition to the universe of beings. Rather, it thinks of God (or "the sacred" or "Spirit," terms which I use interchangeably and synonymously) as a non-material level or layer or dimension of reality that pervades the universe. To use William James's generic term for God, God is "the more." "The more" is all around us and within us; the universe is shot through with the presence of God. Thus God and the universe are not completely separate; rather, the universe is "in God," and we, and all that is, are "in God."

Importantly, panentheism does not identify God and the universe. God is not the universe, and the universe is not God. Rather, though the universe is in God, God is more than the universe. Thus "the more" is "right here," intimately present, as well as "more than right here."

Though less familiar than supernatural theism, panentheism is just as ancient and just as Christian. It is found throughout the scriptures and sacred traditions of the enduring religions, including the Bible and Christianity. One of the central claims of Karen Armstrong's best-seller *A History of God* is that these two ways of thinking about God are found side by side in the three Abrahamic religions (Judaism, Christianity, and Islam) from their ancient beginnings to the present day.

As a concept of God, panentheism has several virtues. It resolves the intellectual difficulties posed by thinking of God as a being "out there." It also removes the intellectual difficulties posed by the notion of divine intervention. The interventionist model of the God-world relation, associated with supernatural theism, presumes that God is normally "not here" but "out there," and acts "here" only through intervention. But because panentheism affirms that God is "right here," it rejects the interventionist model and affirms instead an "intentional" and "interactive" model of the God-world relation. It speaks not of divine intervention, but divine intention and divine interaction.

Panentheism not only resolves the intellectual difficulties posed by supernatural theism, but also changes how we think of prayer. Prayer is no longer about beseeching a being "out there" who may or may not exist, but is far more intimate. It is about centering ever more deeply in "the more" who is "right here," the one in whom we live and move and have our being. It is also about seeking to align ourselves with God's intention and opening ourselves to divine interaction.

For me as for many people in our time, panentheism has made it possible to take the reality of God seriously again. And yet in most of our churches, the language of worship and prayer continues to be dominated by the language of supernatural theism. As I mentioned earlier, it is the natural language of worship and prayer, and there is nothing wrong with it so long as it is not literalized or semi-literalized.

We need another language to guard against such literalization and the problems it creates. Hence the importance of this book: its prayers to a panen-theistic God provide prayer language that affirms

that the sacred is right here close at hand, intimate.
The word "God" does not refer to a being who may
or may not exist, but to the reality, the sacred
mystery, within which we live.

We need both languages. The language of
supernatural theism, the language of personifying
God, reminds us that God is personal and that we
can have a personal relationship with God. The
language of panentheism reminds us that God is
not "a person" "somewhere else" (and perhaps not
at all). Rather, it speaks of God, the sacred, "the
more," as the sea of being all around us and within
us. We are in God as fish are in water.

To use a biblical metaphor that makes the same
point: in the Bible, in both Hebrew and Greek, the
same word is used for wind, breath, and Spirit. The
language of panentheism affirms that God, the
Spirit, is the wind around us and the breath within
us. We live within the Spirit, even as the Spirit is the
life-force within us.

Though this way of thinking about God is
relatively unfamiliar, it really shouldn't be. Those
of us who grew up in the church have heard it

from childhood. We not only prayed "Our Father who art in heaven," but were also taught that God is "everywhere." When we combine these two affirmations, we have panentheism: God is everywhere present, and yet beyond everything, "right here" and yet "more than right here." The semi-technical language for these two affirmations is the transcendence and immanence of God. When one affirms both, as orthodox Christianity throughout the centuries consistently has, the result is panentheism, whether one calls it this or not.

Panentheism is thus deeply rooted in the Christian tradition. It is not a modern innovation, but orthodox Christianity. And this book helps us to recover this ancient, rich, and persuasive vision of God. It does so by giving us prayer language that expresses this vision by addressing the "You" who is "right here" as well as "more than right here." It will help many Christians to rediscover a life of prayer.

—MARCUS BORG

INTRODUCTION

Each of us has a "religion," that is, a deep-seated worldview—an understanding of reality that is the ground of our perceptions and actions. Our beliefs about the nature of reality color every moment. They can imbue life with a sense of purpose and joy, or deprive it of meaning and infect it with despair.

For thousands of years men and women found meaning and a deep sense of belonging through faith in God. But today, in significant part, ours is a culture of disbelief.[4] The mechanistic viewpoint of classical, Newtonian physics fosters this attitude. From that perspective, we seem to live in a universe of separate objects, interacting solely though physical causes and effects—a world in which there is no room for a transcendent dimension or ultimate meaning.

We tend to accept the Newtonian version because everyday experience appears to confirm it. We think in terms of separately labeled, fixed "things," and we consider ourselves separate from all we observe. Yet we do not really live in a world of unchanging, discrete parts. We live in a world that is in a never-ending state of interconnected movement and change. And although we seem to be detached from the world around us, when we reflect, we realize we are not. We are inseparable from the flowing dynamic of the world.

The revolutions in science that occurred in the last century revealed that reality is infinitely stranger than classical physics assumed. The classical approach does not provide a complete description of the world in which we live.

We have learned that the biosphere and every organism in it—indeed, all of nature—is the product of a dynamic in which the whole is greater than the sum of its parts. Each living thing is an aggregation of millions of microorganisms acting cooperatively in ways that cannot be explained by analysis of its constituents. We have discovered that we do not live in a universe made up of elemental particles of matter, because "matter" itself is a network of relationships.

In the early years of the twentieth century it was widely assumed that eventually we would discover the explanation for the workings of the universe and its origins. Now, in the early years of the twenty-first, we have rediscovered the humbling, ancient truth—that we live in a fathomless and transcendent mystery.

By an inexplicable process, we were brought into life from stardust. Daily it provides us with all the wonders and challenges of existence: spring breezes, loyalty, wildflowers, curiosity, mountains, consciousness, poems, friendship, tragedy, laughter, fear, trust, joy, death, birth, clouds, love, sexuality, tigers, songbirds, struggle, gain, loss, integrity, duplicity, oceans, economic forces, concern, trees, doubt, and faith—in short, with all that is. And when we look deep inside ourselves to discover what we are, we find that the answer to that question is as much an unsolved puzzle as the origin of the universe.

Consider the deep mystery of the present. The instant we turn our attention to it, it is gone. Each moment in time is impossible to hold; yet, the present is always with us. We think of "moments" as if they were discrete, and we think of past, present, and future as if they are separate, but there is no dividing line between them. Time has no separations—it is a seamless flow. Yet the past and the future are never actually with us, they can only be remembered or anticipated from our standpoint in the inexorably moving, yet permanent, present.

The world in which we live is infinite in every direction and in time. Our universe has no edge, yet the notion of an area without a boundary is inconceivable. We have no answer to such questions as: Why does anything exist at all? Scientists may refer to reality, theologians may refer to God, but they speak of the same enigma.

Our collective understanding of the nature of the world has changed over the centuries. And our individual understanding changes as we learn, experience, and grow older. Over the years, my own concept of reality has been reshaped by the discovery of important areas of convergence in the thought of many philosophers, theologians, biologists, physicists, chemists, and neuro-scientists.[5]

For the main part, the ideas suggested by these sources appear to me to be consistent with a viewpoint that philosophers and theologians call "pan*en*theism." The noted essayist Annie Dillard reports that panentheism "is the private view of most Christian intellectuals today."[6] But it is, by no means, limited to Christians.[7] The term distinguishes a way of thinking about the Ultimate from both pantheism and theism.

Today's panentheists believe the material universe is ultimate reality—that it is a self-created, self-contained, meaningless system of physical causes and effects. Traditional theists assert that God is transcendent, perfect, unchanging, omnipotent, and separate from the ever-changing world—that God is away, removed from us. This is the concept of God that I was taught as a child. Many find that depiction inconsistent with reality. Others, while accepting it, find such a God too abstract and remote to make any real impact in their lives.

The panentheist perception is that God or Reality or whatever name we use is both an incomprehensible mystery—transcending the universe and all our ideas, including our ideas of time and space and our ideas of God—*and* God permeates the evolving and changing processes of the world and ourselves. Thus: *pan*, all; *en*, in; *theos*, God. In theological terminology, God is both immanent and transcendent.

Of course, there are numerous ways to envision the Absolute, and every description, however dear to us, is only metaphor. The most common metaphor for God in the West is that of God as father. The Bible uses many different images. Psalm 18 portrays God as a rock, deliverer, fortress, high tower, judge, and protector. Other metaphors for God found in the Bible include light, spirit, shepherd, lawgiver, breath, healer, friend, fire, and as a woman giving birth. In some Eastern traditions, the Ultimate is thought of as the Void;

in others, the Way. Different images speak to different people, since we each co-create the reality in which we live.

God, whom the scientists call the whole of reality—whom Saint Augustine called the *aliud valde*, the Hindus called *anyad eva*, and Jewish mystics called *Ein Sof*—the God who transcends our thoughts of God, who, in the words of Paul's letter to the Ephesians, "is above all, and through all, and in us all," cannot be reduced to mathematical formulas, to philosophy, to creeds, or to words. Thus the Torah prohibited speaking the holy name. Thus the admonition by the Chinese sage, Lao Tzu, in the first verse of the *Tao Te Ching*: "He who speaks does not know." Thus the cautions more recently expressed by twentieth-century philosopher Ludwig Wittgenstein: "What can be said at all can be said clearly; and whereof one cannot speak thereof one must be silent."

Just as all scientific knowledge is provisional, so is all human knowledge of the nature of the Ultimate. No doubt all our ideas of the Absolute are further removed from definitive truth than a trout's perceptions are removed from Einstein's. Our thoughts and expressions are inherently inadequate attempts to express something about existence in an endless, ever present unknown. Since at best we see only a part of ultimate truth, we must be tolerant of the views of others and intolerant of intolerance.

Although we are locked in what Friedrich Nietzsche called a "prison house of language," in which all our thoughts, our creeds, our theologies, our scientific theories, and our mathematical formulas are imperfect metaphors for the Actual, we cannot think or communicate without symbols. Because the symbols we accept form the lenses through which we perceive the world, we continually look for those that bring us closer to Truth. And the symbols we accept have consequences. This is especially, and often tragically, the case with our symbols for the cause of being. Men and women have given their lives and have tortured and killed one another to preserve and to propagate their conceptions of the Divine.

I have been attracted to the concepts of

panentheism because, for me, they seem closer to Truth than others. The panentheist account has significant implications. In my view they include these:

- ◆ When one says, "I believe in God," it means, "I believe that the Unconditional, the Ultimate, the Divine, is present in all, and is All—all of life, all persons, all creatures, all the universe, *and* I believe that there is more than we can perceive or comprehend, a dimension beyond the apparent world of time and space."

- ◆ The commandment to "love God with all your heart, with all your mind, and with all your strength" is understood to mean that we are to "love creation, experience, and the radical mystery that is at its center, with all our heart, with all our mind, and with all our strength."

- ◆ The knowledge that God is present in all our fellow beings explains why the commandment to love God is violated when we fail to love our neighbor.

- The understanding that God pervades the eternal and relentlessly moving present offers us the opportunity to recognize the constant Presence in the miracle of daily life.
- Increases in human knowledge are understood as a part of God's continuing revelation.
- To be "saved" is to fully incorporate into our lives the fact that we are one with and expressions of God. Our vulnerability and insignificance, even our fear of death, are swept away by the knowledge that we are not only the instruments through whom the music of the Infinite is played—we are the Symphony.
- "Sin" is the result of our forming an erroneous relationship with God and the world. It consists of giving one's primary devotion to something other than the truly Ultimate.
- This world can be the kingdom of God, because our world is a world balanced between freedom and order, within which

our choices co-create our experience; we
may, by those choices, make it into the
kingdom of God.

◆ The essence of religion is not belief; it is a
way of living. As Saint Augustine said in the
Enchiridion: "For when we ask how good a
person is, we do not ask what they believe or
what they hope for, but what they live."

◆ Meditation and prayer are means of
becoming conscious of "the Beyond in our
midst." Worship services provide us the
opportunity to be reminded of the "good
news" that we live in the Divine. They assist
us to discover that the Holy is always with
us, if we will only awake to it.

◆ We say "God is love" to express the intimacy
of our relationship with God, but God's
relationship to us is even closer than love,
because God is more than a separate being
who loves us—we are an indivisible part of
God.

◆ For Christians, the life of Jesus exemplifies
the profoundly deep, selfless life to which

we should aspire; and Christ's resurrection occurs today when we give life to compassion and love—the expressions of the universal Christ within.

These intuitions suggest fertile ways to think of God as:

- The creative consciousness expressed in history, in evolution, and in our minds at this very moment;
- The intelligence in every organized system, from simple molecules to the human brain;
- The process of giving and receiving love and compassion;
- The spirit behind the eyes of every living being;
- The network of relationships forming the material world;
- Not "he," not "she," not "it," and yet inclusive of all these;
- The eternal, ungraspable, ever changing "Now";
- The living process, articulated by all creation, "who" or "which" cannot be encompassed by our words or even by our thoughts—because

our every idea is an unfolding aspect of the transcendent mystery we call "God"—but for which we have no adequate name.

And what are the implications of these concepts to the age-old question: Is God responsible for evil and tragedy? The difficulty in answering it stems from the assumption that God is an omnipotent being who dictates all that happens. But if that were so, our apparent freedom to choose would be an illusion. Because I believe that I am free to choose, I accept the panentheist view that the God "in whom we live and move and have our being" (Acts 17:28) is not an omnipotent, controlling being, but is evolving and changing as we, and the world, evolve and change. And as a being living in God, as a manifestation of God, my freedom to shape the way I perceive the world and my freedom to act in compassionate or selfish ways places co-responsibility on me. It follows that the Day of Judgment is today, when I assess my actions and my failures to act.

What use have I made of these challenging ideas? I have learned from long experience that engaging in the daily practice of meaningful reading, prayer, meditation, and reflection is vital if I am to replace my day-to-day mindset with a deeper vision. In order to incorporate these understandings into my daily routine, I prepared two weeks of morning and evening meditations using those concepts. I drew on the Bible for a foundation, but I did not limit myself to quotations. My objective was an interpretation, not a reproduction.

I am an Episcopalian and I was raised using the Anglican Book of Common Prayer. (For those unfamiliar with that work, it is a collection of worship services used by Anglicans throughout the world. Most religious groups have some form of analogous liturgy.) In my tradition those services are not just used in church. We are encouraged to use them in private daily worship. To determine if the use of panentheist metaphors would enliven my own religious heritage, I also rewrote four Anglican services. My purpose in rewriting the services was to provide material for private reading and reflection. Since they are based on forms of corporate worship from the Book of Common

Prayer, I suppose they could be used for corporate worship, but I did not write them with that in mind.

One of the services was Holy Communion or Eucharist. Because it is the most revered service in my tradition, I made no attempt to deal with the events of the Last Supper or the sacrifice of Jesus, which are central to that service. I gave that restated service a different name to distinguish it. Another was the Burial of the Dead. I made it into a memorial service that could be used in a way analogous to the Jewish tradition of "sitting Shiva," taking time out to remember and honor the departed.

As I revised the services and prepared the daily meditations, I found that it was unnecessary to abandon all traditional wording because there are numerous Biblical passages that speak of God in a panentheist sense. One of the surprises of this exercise was how close the restatements came to the traditional. Although the panentheist perspective did not require it, I substituted other terms for God in the passages referring to God as "He," "Lord," or "Father" because, for me, they were too suggestive of God as an "old man in the sky."

There are those who will be disturbed by my effrontery in altering some of the majestic poetry of the Book of Common Prayer and the Bible. But this was not written for those who find complete reassurance in the male, humanlike image of God that is dominant in those two works. It was written for women and men like myself, for whom the combined effect of the Newtonian, mechanistic worldview and the inability to accept the conventional image of God as an omnipotent being out there somewhere produced a fear (and, at times, a conviction) that there is no larger, deeper dimension to our lives.

It is my custom to give myself a few minutes each morning and some evenings (I am inconsistent in my practice in the evenings) for meaningful reading, followed by prayer or reflection and by a few minutes of quiet. I have used readings from the Bible, the Book of Common Prayer, poetry, theology, philosophy, physics, and a wide variety of spiritual writers from every major religion. The readings help to spark some comprehension of life's deeper dimension. If I am using a prayer, sometimes I pray the prayer; at other times, I just read it. At times, I read silently; at other times, aloud. Afterwards I am quiet for a few minutes. The prayers and the readings are the tools I use to set the stage for the silence.

After writing these revised prayers and services, I used them in my customary ways. One welcome effect of using alternative descriptions for the Absolute was that I was returned to my religious roots with a new appreciation. Another was that I discovered that one metaphor was particularly helpful to me. Thinking of God as the infinite mystery manifested in the Present, as the Eternal directly revealed in the inexplicable and indivisible Now, which is always changing but never ceases to be, awakened me to the immediacy and power of the Divine in a deeper and more intimate way.

However, even though these words were closer to my perception of God than the traditional, words were not enough. This came as no surprise. Opening myself to the presence of the "Beyond in our midst" requires more than words. It calls for something that may be impossible to communicate in words—an internal receptiveness—the receipt of a grace. As Saint Augustine said: "Before experiencing God you thought you could talk about God; when you begin to experience God you realize that what you are experiencing you cannot put into words."[8]

From time to time, when I am able to find the right internal note, these intuitions help me to experience the *knowledge,* not the mere intellectual belief, that, as Meister Eckhart said seven centuries ago, "we swim in a sea of God."

My ideas of God will almost certainly not be yours. My hope for you, the reader, is not that you will adopt the metaphors that appeal to me, but that this experiment will invite you to consider those you have accepted. What is your real "religion," your deep-seated worldview? And what is its effect on your life?

AN EXPRESSION
OF FAITH

We have faith that the whole of reality is God
    relating to God,
That we are to God as a wave is to the sea.
God is the thinker and the thought,
The force of gravity,
The wind on the waters,
The process of change,
The air we breathe,
The water we drink,
The bread we eat.

God is the nameless origin of names,
Acting in all that is,
Evolving and changing,
Uncreated, Ultimate, Unfathomable,
From whom all things proceed,
Of which all things are,

To which all things return.

God is the universe that has no edge,
The morning dew and the center of the sun,
God between us,
God beyond us,
God breathes us.
Rising, increasing, changing,
The great miracle and enigma,
Outside all categories,
The relationship of all relationships,
The medium of all communication,
The cause of love and love itself.
God in ourselves, our souls and bodies.

God is the source of time and endless time itself.
God is the present moment,
The Now that never ceases to be,
Infinite in all directions.

God fills the universe,
And the kingdom of God is within us.
If we could conceive all the worlds that exist,
They would be less than God's kingdom,

The place of freedom from place,
The time of freedom from time.

God is the smile on a loved one's face,
The gift of friendship,
The shared laughter that brightens the day,
Compassion and care offered during tragedy
    and joy.
God is the sleeping spirit of Christ present in
    every heart,
Ready to rise from the dead in each act of
    loving-kindness.

We trust that if we have true humility,
Which is the courage to abandon self-concern
    and fear,
We will experience the joy of self-transcendence,
And the peace that passes all understanding.

For the Holy is always with us, if we will
    awake to it.
It is the unwavering, constant embrace.
It is not a state of being.
It is not a state of mind.

It is that within which all states come and go.
For there are no words to describe the Presence,
It is the words we speak,
The sky we breathe,
The world we see,
The eyes through which we see,
And the eternal awareness behind our eyes.

A CYCLE OF DAILY OFFICES

WEEK ONE

SUNDAY MORNING

The Morning Greeting

How lovely is this, your dwelling place,
Mystery of mysteries.
How I long for awareness of your company.
How I rejoice when I feel your companionship.
The sparrow finds his home in you,
The swallow builds her nest in your branches
Where she may lay her young in your arms.
Blessed are those who are aware
That they dwell in you,
For they fill their days with peace.
A minute awake to your presence
Is better than a thousand days alone.

PSALM 84[9]

A Reading from Scripture

For I am sure that neither death, nor life,
Nor angels, nor principalities,
Nor things present, nor things to come,
Nor powers, nor height, nor depth,
Nor anything else in all creation,
Can separate us from the love of God.

ROMANS 8:38–39

A Meditation

"Your enjoyment of the world is never right,
Till every morning you awake in Heaven."

THOMAS TRAHERNE[10]

The Concluding Prayer

Enveloping spirit,
We thank you for this priceless day, which will
    never come again.
Through it, you offer us
The opportunity to fill it with compassion and joy.
Help us to trust in your unfolding grace
And transcend self-concern,
So that at this very moment, and throughout this
    day,

We may live fearlessly and generate loving-
    kindness,
And thereby experience the only true wealth,
That of life in you.
Amen.

SUNDAY EVENING

The Words of Assurance.

To whom will you liken God?
What image could you contrive?
Who could be the equal of the Divine?
Lift up your eyes and look.
Who made the stars?

                                    ISAIAH 40

A Reading from Scripture
Great is our God above all gods.
For who is able to comprehend God,
Since the heaven and heaven of heavens,
Cannot contain the mystery of our being?

                        2 CHRONICLES 2:5–6

A Reading

I came forth from beyond this world,
And I covered the earth like a mist.
I had my tent in the heights,
And my throne in the clouds.
Over the sea and the earth I searched for rest,
And looked to see where I might pitch my tent.
Then I pitched my tent in humankind.
Now I am like a vine putting out graceful shoots,
Approach me and take your fill of my fruits.
They who eat of me will hunger no more,
Whoever drinks of me will thirst no more.
From eternity I came,
And for eternity I will remain.

ECCLESIASTICUS 24

The Concluding Prayer

Infinite reality,
Unending in time,
Unending in every direction,
You surround us,
You pervade us.
Everywhere we look,
There you are.

We swim in a sea that is made of you.
Our every cell is made of you.
Lift every concern from our hearts,
For we are filled with your being.
Give us awareness that always and everywhere,
We rest in you,
Now and forever.
Amen.

MONDAY MORNING

The Promise for the Morning
I will lift the stone from your heart,
And a new spirit I will put within you.

EZEKIEL 36:26

Morning Invocation
Sing a new song,
Rejoice in our days,
And dance in praise.
For the Timeless is present in every moment,
And takes pleasure in our joy.

PSALM 149

Psalm

Make a joyful noise,
Serve with gladness,
Respond with song.
For Life is holy.
The Divine Mystery has made us,
And not we ourselves.
We are God's people, creatures of the Infinite.
Live this day with pleasure,
And be thankful,
For the embrace of the Eternal
Endures to all generations.

PSALM 100

The Concluding Prayer

Life-giver,
Where I am,
You are.
What I feel,
You feel.
What I think,
You think.
So transparent is my unity with you
That my eye and your eye

Are one eye and one seeing
And one knowing and one loving.
In awe I confess:
That what I do,
You do.
Assist me this day to be worthy
Of you.
Amen.

MONDAY EVENING

The Evening Psalm
The wind is your messenger,
The clouds are your chariots.
The earth rests in you,
And springs gush from your mountains.
The cedars of Lebanon you planted,
In them, the birds settle in their nests.
The wild goats roam your mountains.
In the rocky crags, badgers hide.
You made the moon to tell the seasons.
While you bring darkness on,
The lions seek their prey.

The vast expanse of ocean
Teems with countless life.
All creatures exist in you.
What endless variety you are.

Psalm 104

The Concluding Prayer

You unfold this world from another dimension,
Each moment you bring all of creation into
    being,
Again and again we receive your gifts.
Mystery at the center of all,
Your universe is a daily miracle.
Endow us now, at the end of the day
With the sense of your presence.
Bestow on us peace as we prepare to rest,
And bring us into awareness
That we are part of your timeless kingdom,
Now and forever.
Amen.

TUESDAY MORNING

The Morning Greeting

Omnipresent Consciousness,
You look out through my eyes
And the eyes of friends and family.
You know when I sit
And when I rise,
You discern my thoughts.
You are acquainted with all my ways.
Before a word is on my tongue,
You know it.
You surround me behind and before,
My hands themselves are yours.
Such knowledge is too wonderful for me,
It is too high,
I cannot attain it.
Where shall I go from your spirit?
Where can I flee from your presence?
If I ascend into the sky, you are there.
If I lie in the grave, you are there.
If I take the wings of the morning
Or dwell in the uttermost parts of the sea,

Even there you shall lead me.
If I say, "Let darkness cover me,
Let the light be night,"
The darkness is not dark to you,
The night is as bright as the day.
For you knit me together in my mother's womb,
Fearful and wonderful is your nature.
You formed the days for me,
When there were no days.

PSALM 139

The Concluding Prayer

Eternal Progression,
You, who express me at this instant,
Open my heart during this day.
Help me to be continuously thankful,
And to share your love with all I touch this day.
For I seek to fully trust in your grace.
Therefore, without reservation, as this day
    begins,
I let go of the cares of the world,
And gratefully and joyfully accept
The overwhelming gift of being.
Amen.

TUESDAY EVENING

~

The Words of Assurance for Evening

The Never-ending is my light and my salvation:
Whom shall I fear?
The Eternal within me is the strength of my life:
Of whom shall I be afraid?
Though a host should encamp against me,
My heart shall not tremble.
Though war should rise up in opposition to me,
In the embrace of the Unlimited will I be confident.
When my father and mother forsake me,
The Source of all will fill me up.
In the midst of my enemies, the Comforter shall
    envelope me.
I will be of good courage because the Infinite
    is in me.

PSALM 27

The Concluding Prayer

Incomprehensible Mystery,
Here in this instant and always,
Deep within our being,

From the dust of stars
You brought us into existence,
And provided this day.
From the moment of birth,
You have sheltered us from death.
As night falls,
Help us, in your grace,
To be thankful,
And to make our lives worthy of your gifts.
Amen.

WEDNESDAY MORNING

The Promise
Fear not, for I am with thee.

ISAIAH 43:5

A Morning Canticle
Before the oldest of my works,
From the timeless I was.
Before the earth came into being,
Before the mountains were settled,
Before the beginning,

I was there.
There were no springs to gush forth,
Yet I was there.
There were no mountains,
Yet I was there.
My delight is in you day after day,
And through you I am at play.
I delight in the children of all people.
Happy are those who keep my ways,
For those who find me find life.

PROVERBS 8

A Meditation

In life we are in grace.
In every moment and in every place
We live suspended in the web of Divinity of
    which we are made.
Therefore, we leave our fears and concerns
    behind,
And place our complete trust in the Infinite.
We rest in the never-ending embrace.
We merge our spirits with your spirit
And with one another in the mystical delight in
    our world.

We call forth from within ourselves the spirit of
    the Christ within,
Of forgiveness and unconditional
    compassion,
We offer Christ's kindness to one another.

The Concluding Prayer

Inexhaustible Unity,
Your origin is our origin,
We are an outpouring of your grace.
Therefore, as we begin this day,
We place our complete trust in you.
Help us to merge our spirits with your spirit,
To live as you live,
Without the need for justification,
To live life as an end and not a means,
And to find within ourselves
Christ's empathy, resurrected and incarnate,
In this place and time.
So that today, unreservedly,
We may offer care and compassion
To every person with whom we come in
    contact.
Amen.

WEDNESDAY EVENING

The Words of Assurance
Jesus said:
The kingdom of God is not found by
    observation:
We cannot say, look here! Or look there!
For the kingdom of God is within you.

LUKE 17:20–21

A Meditation
Limitless center of our being,
You are our refuge and strength,
Therefore we will not fear.
Though the earth be moved,
Though the mountains are carried into the sea.
You are the river in which every stream is joined,
The beyond in our midst
From which we can never be parted.
People rage, kingdoms are destroyed,
But when we open ourselves to you, all that is
    earthly melts away.
Then our conflicts shall cease, and our weapons
    will be broken.

Psalm

Be still and know
That God is with us.

PSALM 46

The Concluding Prayer

Inexhaustible Power,
Your kingdom encompasses the universe.
Yet if we could conceive of all the worlds that
     exist,
The stars in their courses,
The galaxies without number,
They would be less than your kingdom within us:
The place of freedom from place,
The time of freedom from time.

As this day ends, we thank you for allowing us
The priceless gift of experiencing this marvelous
     world.
May the thanks we express with our lips
Reflect the thanks we feel in our hearts.
Amen.

THURSDAY MORNING

The Words of Promise
Am I not a God at hand, and not a God afar off?
Can any hide himself in secret places that I shall
    not see him?
Do I not fill heaven and earth?
                                    JEREMIAH 23:24

Holy Spirit expressing the world,
Assist me to awake this day and realize,
    as Jacob did,
That "God is in this place and I knew it not."
                                    GENESIS 28:16

Psalm
Divine Unifier of endless time with infinite space,
The heavens declare your glory,
And the earth displays your handiwork.
Day after day reveals your beauty,
And night after night your endless reach.
There is no speech, nor are there words, to
    encompass you,
Immortal Continuity,

Your consciousness extends throughout
     our universe
And beyond.

PSALM 1:1–4

The Concluding Prayer

Unwavering Presence,
As I awake I seek your peace.
Birds sing throughout the world,
The ocean washes countless shores,
Clouds move across the skies,
And you are here in all of this.
I open my heart to you this day.
Since before the beginning of time
You are Emmanuel, "God with us."
You fill my being.
The eyes with which I see your creation
Are the eyes through which you see.
There is nothing for me to gain,
Nothing for me to lose.
I look at the sky,
There you are.
I consider my hands,
There you are.
Amen.

THURSDAY EVENING

The Evening Psalm

Life Creator
Life Sustainer,
Life Taker,
In you are life and death itself.
Teach me to number my days,
That I may know how to live fully.
You have made my days a few handbreadths,
My time is nothing in your sight.
I amass riches and I know not who will gather.
For what do I wait?
My existence is in you.

PSALM 39

The Concluding Prayer

Hidden Still Point,
You offer us
The continual power of renewal,
The ability to be restored in sleep.
Therefore, as we prepare for rest,
We let go of every fear,
We abandon every concern.

We place our trust in your Spirit.
So that as we end this day,
And at the last,
We may share in your timeless joy:
Free from sorrow, regret, and fear,
Resting in the knowledge
That all of reality is God's relationship with God.
Amen.

FRIDAY MORNING

The Words of Promise
Jesus said:
I tell you solemnly,
Whatever you did to the least of these,
You did to me.

MATTHEW 25:40

The Morning Prayer
Spirit of companionship and caring,
We express heartfelt gratitude
For the company of our friends and family,
Through whom we experience your gift of love.
Help us to break the bonds of self-concern,

And to extend to all those with whom we come in
    contact
The priceless riches of compassion and empathy,
So that in our time,
They and we may truly experience the heaven you offer,
Through the power of the Christ within.
Amen.

The Concluding Prayer
Sacred Unknown,
You called us into existence,
You feed us from the land's rich soil.
Daily you offer us renewal.
We thank you for the living earth,
Of which we are a part,
And for our friends and family, who nurture us.
We place our trust in you,
So that in this life,
We may share in your timeless joy:
Free from sorrow, regret, and fear,
Living the message of the Christ within:
The way to full and fearless life
Is to transcend self-concern for ourselves.
Amen.

Friday Evening

The Evening Psalm

Celestial Unity,
You are our resting place
From one generation to another.
Before the mountains were brought forth,
Before you formed the earth and the sky, you are.
A thousand years in your sight
Are as a watch in the night.
You sweep us away
Like grass that is green in the morning,
And in the evening is cut down and withers.
For our days pass away,
And our years come to an end like a sigh.
Teach us to number our days
So we may apply our hearts to wisdom.

Psalm 90

The Concluding Prayer

Living God,
You are the continuous creative event.
I came from you,
I live in you,

I will die in you.
You are every thought I have,
And my every experience.
You rest behind my eyes
And in the clouds above.
You are the night sky,
The waves on the dark waters,
And the medium in which they move.
You are the source of my consciousness
And my awareness itself.
Throughout this day you preserved me
For a purpose I need not understand.
Assist me to see you in all,
And to be worthy of your gifts.
Amen.

SATURDAY MORNING

Morning Psalm
For God alone my soul waits in silence.
My hope is in God:
My deliverer, my rock,
My salvation.
People of low and high estate are but a breath,

Their status is a delusion.
If wealth increases, put no store in it.
All power belongs to God,
And God is steadfast love.
We are requited,
According to the life we create.

PSALM 62

A Scripture Reading

Love your enemies,
Do good to those who hate you,
Bless those who curse you,
Pray for those who mistreat you,
And you will be the children of God.
Be compassionate.
Do not judge and you will not be judged,
Give and you will be given gifts,
Forgive and you will receive forgiveness.
For you are made in God's image,
A co-creator of your world.
Thus, that which you give is that which you will
    obtain.

LUKE 6:27, 35–38

The Concluding Prayer

Living Center of our being,
Through the message of Jesus
And the teachings of those who have come
    before us,
We have learned that transformed existence is
    always possible
When we sincerely attempt to live lives of
    loving-kindness
And accept forgiveness for past failures.
Give us the courage, as this day begins,
To accept forgiveness now
For every wrong that we have done this day;
Not as an abstract assertion,
But as an essential encounter with your
    creative power,
And the means of beginning anew.
We desire not the false happiness of this
    world,
But the authentic peace of the blessed,
The comfort of remembering that we are
Always and everywhere,
Aspects of you.
Amen.

SATURDAY EVENING

A Psalm of Assurance for Evening
Divine Center,
You are our refuge and strength,
Therefore we will not fear.
Though the earth be moved,
Though the mountains are carried into the sea.
You are the river in which every stream is joined,
From which we can never be parted.
Men rage, their kingdoms are destroyed,
But when we lose ourselves in you,
All that is earthly melts away.
Then our conflicts shall cease,
And our weapons will be broken.
Be still and know
That you are with us.

PSALM 46

The Concluding Prayer
Holy and Immortal,
Beyond at the center of all,
Remind us of our mortality,

So that we may enter fully into the present.
Ground us in the reality of your eternal now,
So that we may completely live each moment.
Allow your divinity to penetrate us,
And teach us to rest in you,
Not as a fleeting experience,
But as a way of being.
As sleep takes us into another dimension,
Assist us to trust completely in your eternal
    unfolding.
Amen.

A CYCLE OF
DAILY OFFICES
WEEK TWO

SUNDAY MORNING

~

A Reading from Scripture

Let the same mind
Be in us,
That was in Christ Jesus.

PHILIPPIANS 2:5

Morning Canticle

Praise the Everlasting and Holy.
Take joy in the miracle of creation,
For we live in the mystery of the Unbounded,
In this marvelous world we are alive.
Sing praises to the most Holy,
For life is given to us.
Take pleasure in reality's gifts,

Creation is wonder filled,
The foundation of being surpasses all our
    thoughts.
In earth, in the seas,
And in the deepest places,
The Infinite makes the clouds to rise at the end of
    the sky.
The Absolute makes the lightning and the rain.
The idols of people are but the work of human
    hands.
Praise the eternal Now,
God with us endures forever.

PSALM 135

The Concluding Prayer

Holy, never-ending One,
As I enter this marvelous day,
I place my trust in you,
Mystery of mysteries,
Beyond any name or thought,
Who brought me into being,
And sustains me this moment.
The living God,
The continuous creative event

Transcending human thought,
Out of which I came,
In which I live,
Assist me this day
To see past our apparent separations,
And to perceive the unity of all your creatures.
Amen.

SUNDAY EVENING

The Words of Assurance for Eventide
I dwell in the shelter of the most High,
The Divine Unity
Is my refuge.
I will not be afraid of any terror this night
Nor of any sickness that stalks the darkness.
I have made the Infinite my refuge,
The most High my habitation.
Because God is bound to me in love,
With full life and complete trust will I please
    my Creator.

PSALM 9

A Meditation

When we abandon the illusion that we are
    separated from God,
The difference between the time when we are here
And the time before we were is no longer
    meaningful,
And the difference between the time when we
    are here
And the time when we will be gone dissipates.
When we understand that we are the breath of
    the Infinite,
Time and existence no longer limit us.

The Concluding Prayer

In life we are in grace.
In every moment and in every place,
We live suspended in the web of Divinity
    which we are.
Therefore, we leave our fears and concerns
    behind,
And place our complete trust in the Infinite.
We rest in the never-ending Presence.
We merge our spirits with the Spirit
In the mystical delight in our world.

We call forth from within ourselves
The spirit of the Christ within,
The spirit of forgiveness,
The spirit of unconditional compassion.

MONDAY MORNING

Morning Promise
If you do away with the desire to use others,
With the clenched fist, the wicked word,
If you give your bread to the hungry,
And relief to the oppressed,
Your light shall shine in the darkness,
And your shadow shall be as noon.
The spirit of the Transcendent will always be
    alive in you.
You will be like a spring
Whose waters never run dry.

ISAIAH 58:7–12

Psalm
Do not fret about the wicked,
Do not envy those who benefit from wrong,

For they wither like grass which lacks water.
Trust in the Creative Process,
And do good,
For those who do good dwell in the Divine,
And great is that reward.
Commit your ways to the Eternal, and it shall
    come to pass.
Be quiet in the bosom of God, rest there,
Do not trouble yourself with those who scheme.
Cease from anger, forsake wrath,
For evildoers cut themselves off from their
    endowment,
The only inheritance worth a lifetime.
The wicked limit their lives with their own
    actions,
For the internal treasure of a childlike pauper
Is greater than the greatest fortune.

PSALM 37

The Concluding Prayer

Ever present Reality,
As I go about this day's commerce,
And meet with this day's challenges,
I ask that you awaken in me

The joy of self-transcendence,
And the knowledge and experience that we are,
Always and everywhere,
Aspects of you,
Unlimited and Eternal One.
Amen.

MONDAY EVENING

An Evening Blessing
One ceaseless Source of all,
Above all, through all,
And in us all.

EPHESIANS 4:6

Psalm
In you, encompassing Presence, have I taken
    refuge;
Let me never be put to shame;
Deliver me in your righteousness.
Into your hands I commend my spirit,
For you have redeemed me,
God of all.

PSALM 31:1, 5

The Concluding Prayer
Limitless Depth,
Tonight, as I shed the events of the day,
I seek to free myself of everything that blocks me
    from you.
Empty of every want,
Empty of every need,
Empty of desire to be anything but what I am,
Here in this moment of the eternal Now,
Efficiency and purpose are set aside.
I do not possess.
I do not strive.
I rest in you.
Amen.

TUESDAY MORNING

The Morning Invocation
The heaven and heaven of heavens
Cannot contain thee,
How much less this house that I have built?
                    1 KINGS 8:27

A Meditation

Though we speak much, we cannot reach the
    end,
And the sum of all our words is:
You are the All.
For you are greater than your creation.

SIRACH 43:27–28

A Reading from Scripture

For my thoughts are not your thoughts,
Neither are your ways my ways.
For as the heavens are higher than the earth,
So are my ways higher than your ways,
And my thoughts higher than your thoughts.

ISAIAH 55:8–9

Psalm

Be thankful for the incomprehensibility of this
    life,
Take joy in the miracle of creation,
We live in the arms of the Infinite,
In this spectacular world we are alive.
Lift up your hearts,
For life is given to us

To take pleasure in Reality's gifts.
Creation unfolds in every instant,
Our God surpasses all the gods humankind
    might conceive.
In earth, in the seas,
And in the deepest places,
The Unbounded makes the clouds to rise at
    the end of the sky,
The Absolute makes the lightning and the
    rain.
Praise the eternal Now.
Emmanuel, God with us, endures forever.

PSALM 135

The Thanksgiving

Our consciousness is yours,
Inexplicable Foundation.
We give you thanks for creating in us the
    ability to question,
By which facility we have discovered that every
    aspect of creation,
However large or small, is unlimited.
We give you thanks for the ability to perceive
    this world from many points of view,

And for the capacity to sense, through the activity
of our minds,
Your inexhaustible nature.
Amen.

TUESDAY EVENING

An Evening Invocation
For I am sure that neither death, nor life,
Nor angels, nor principalities, nor things present,
Nor things to come, nor powers,
Nor height, nor depth, nor anything else in all
creation,
Can separate us from the love of God.

ROMANS 8:38–39

Psalm
For as great as the stars are high over the earth,
So is your steadfast love.
Our days are like grass.
We flourish like wildflowers,
Then the wind passes over

And we are no more.
But your love
Is everlasting.

PSALM 103

The Concluding Prayer
As the earth moves to hide the sun,
And the distant stars begin to appear,
I set aside all my grievances,
I discard all that is petty,
And I seek the Holy Comforter
At the core of my being.
I wait upon the Living Presence
Deep within me.
Amen.

WEDNESDAY MORNING

Morning Greeting
Do not store up material treasure,
Which moth and rot corrupt,
And thieves steal.
But store up heavenly treasure,

Which neither rust nor moth can corrupt,
And thieves cannot steal.

MATTHEW 6:19–21

A Reading from Scripture

Holy, holy, holy, is the God of our fathers and
    mothers,
The whole universe is full of God's glory.

ISAIAH 6:3

The Concluding Prayer

Endless Multiplicity,
We give thanks for the deep blue of the sky,
The violin's music, the green of the forest,
The enveloping fog, the reflection of clouds on
    still water,
The bird's song, the shade of trees,
And the warmth of the sun.
We see and hear you in all these experiences and
    more,
And for them we give thanks.
Assist us today to respond to you
By opening our hearts to all our fellow beings.
Amen.

WEDNESDAY EVENING

Words of Assurance
Be still and know that I am God.

PSALM 46:10

Evening Meditation
Here in this moment of the eternal Now
We set aside all our cares,
We let go of self-concern,
We abandon all images of the Divine,
We still our hearts and minds,
We experience the eternal Presence,
We join in the mystery of our union with
    Eternity.
We seek to be truly thankful for the joys of
    existence,
And to trust in your grace without reservation.
You unfold this world from another dimension,
Each moment you bring all of creation into
    being,
Again and again we receive your gifts.
Mystery at the center of All,

Your universe is a daily miracle.
Endow us now, at the end of the day
With the sense of your presence.
Bestow on us peace as we prepare to rest,
And bring us into awareness
That we are part of your timeless kingdom,
Now and forever.
Amen.

THURSDAY MORNING

Morning Words of Promise
Thus says the Mystery who created you:
I am with you.
When you walk through fire
You will not be burned.
When you pass through the waters
I will be with you.
You are precious in my sight.
Do not fear, you are mine.

ISAIAH 43:1–2

The Thanksgiving
Hallowed and Unlimited One,
You are beyond us,
Between us,
And within us.
You breathe us.
Rising, increasing, changing,
You are the great miracle,
Outside all our categories,
The relationship of all relationships,
The medium of all communication,
The cause of love and love itself.
You are ourselves, our souls and bodies.
The Now that never ceases to be,
Infinite in time and space,
And more.
Thank you for the gift of this day.
Amen.

THURSDAY EVENING

The Words of Assurance
Fear not, for I am with thee.

ISAIAH 43:5

A Meditation

Immeasurable Spirit,
You brought me into being,
You feed me each day with the products of your
    earth,
Water provided by you courses through me,
Oxygen created by you fills my lungs.
Without the continuous flow of your bounty I
    cannot be.
You are the never-ending Process, and I am your
    creature.

The Concluding Prayer

Infinite Spirit,
You fill my hands, my head, my heart,
You were here before the universe,
You are here now, in my every cell.
Dispel my illusion of separation,
Open my heart, my mind, my being,
To the knowledge
That I am one with you.
Amen.

Friday Morning

~

Words of Promise for the Morning

We are the temple of
The living God, who
Lives and moves in us.

2 Corinthians 6:16

The kingdom of God is not found by observation:
We cannot say look here, or look there.
For the kingdom of God is within you.

Luke 17:20–21

Canticle

I arise today
In power and might,
With trust in the Trinity:
God beyond us,
God between us,
God within us.
I arise today
In love with life,

In hope of rebirth
And gain of Christ's reward.
I place my trust
In the messages of the prophets,
And the good works of the just.
I arise today
With the power of heaven
Under the sun in splendor,
Christ within me:
Christ before me,
Christ behind me,
Christ at my right hand,
Christ on my left,
Christ below and Christ above,
Christ in every ear that hears me,
Christ in every hand that touches me,
Christ in every eye that sees me,
Christ in every heart that thinks of me.
Amen.

BASED ON SAINT PATRICK'S
BREASTPLATE, CA. 390–460

FRIDAY EVENING

The Words of Assurance
For this is to live the life eternal:
To experience our indivisible relationship with
    God.

JOHN 17:3

A Reading from Scripture
God answered Moses and said: "I am Present."

EXODUS 3:14

Evening Meditation
The Sacred is always with us.
It is not found, because it is always here.
It is the Unwavering,
The constant Embrace.
It is not a state of being or a state of mind,
It is the state in which all states come and go.
There are no words to describe the Presence
Because it is the words,
The sky we breathe,
The world we see,

The eyes through which we see,
And the awareness behind our eyes.

The Concluding Prayer
As the gift of another day comes to an end,
We set aside our cares,
We let go of self-concern,
We still our hearts and minds,
We experience the eternal Presence,
We join in the mystery of our union with Eternity
And we abandon ourselves.
And we enter into your peace.
Amen.

SATURDAY MORNING

The Words of Promise
Everyone who abides in love
Abides in God,
And God abides in them.
As God is,
So are we in this world.

There is no fear in love,
For perfect love excludes fear.

I JOHN 4:16–18

The Lord's Prayer

Unfathomable Spring,
Hallowed be your name, which is beyond our
    power to know.
Allow us to experience your heavenly kingdom
    while we are here on earth.
Teach us to be thankful for our daily bread,
Help us to learn that we live in forgiveness to the
    extent we forgive.
And deliver us from self-centered existence.
For we know that only by giving compassion
And living in freedom from selfishness
Will we experience your true kingdom.
Amen.

The Concluding Prayer

Timeless Source of Time,
Life-giving energy,
Through our acts and our thoughts
We take the substance of the universe

And with you we jointly create the world in
    which we live.
Assist us by your grace this day
To make our world a world of compassion and
    forgiveness.
Through the spirit of the Christ within,
Lead us into the joy of fearless life.
Amen.

SATURDAY EVENING

The Words of Assurance
Unlimited Providence is my light and my
    salvation:
Whom shall I fear?
The eternal Spirit within is the strength of
    my life:
Of whom shall I be afraid?
Though a host should encamp against me,
My heart shall not tremble.
Though war should rise up in opposition to me,
In the embrace of the Boundless will I be
    confident.

When all others forsake me,
God supports me.
In the midst of my enemies the Unlimited
    envelops me.
Always and forever I rest in the Divine,
Where God and I are one.
I rest in the grace of the Everlasting.

PSALM 27

Psalm
Yours is the day, O God,
And yours also is the night.
From you came the moon and the stars.

PSALM 74:15

The Concluding Prayer
Infinite Continuity,
Today you used our perceptions to discover the
    world through our eyes;
Everything that occurred was because you were
    unfolding.
Tomorrow we will again be co-creators with you
    of our experiences;
Help us to free ourselves from fear,

To love your creation unreservedly,
And to give ourselves joyfully.
Amen.

A SERVICE OF
MORNING PRAYER

Opening Sentences

Am I not a God at hand, and not a God afar off?
Do not I fill heaven and earth?

JEREMIAH 23:24

For of God, and through God, and to God, are all
    things.

ROMANS 11:36

A Statement of Faith

We have faith that the whole of reality is God
    relating to God,
That we are to God as a wave is to the sea.
God is the thinker and the thought,
The creator and the created,
The force of gravity,
The wind on the waters,

The process of change,
The air we breathe,
The water we drink,
The bread we eat.

God is the nameless origin of names,
Acting in all that is,
Evolving and changing,
Uncreated, ultimate, unfathomable,
From whom all things proceed,
Of which all things are,
To which all things return.

God is the universe that has no edge,
The morning dew and the center of the sun.
God is between us,
God is beyond us,
God is breathing us.
Rising, increasing, changing,
God is the impenetrable enigma,
Outside all categories,
The relationship of all relationships,
The medium of all communication,
The cause of love, and love itself.

God is the source of time and endless time itself,
The present moment,
The eternal now that never ceases to be,
Infinite in all directions.
We are, always and everywhere,
Aspects of the Infinite,
For the kingdom of God is within us;
And if we could conceive all the worlds that exist,
They would be less than God's kingdom,
The place of freedom from place,
The time of freedom from time,
And more.

The Invitation
Teach me, Creative Power,
Give me understanding,
And I shall keep your way.

PSALM 119:33–34

A Summary of the Law
You shall love the eternal Presence,
The never-ending Now,
With all your heart,
With all your soul,

With all your mind,
And with all your strength.
This is the first and greatest commandment.
And the second is the same:
You shall love your neighbor as yourself.
On these two commandments
Hang all the law and the prophets.

MATTHEW 22:37–40

You shall not want anything that is not yours.

EXODUS 20:2–17

The Confession of Sin
We are told by Scripture and tradition to
confront our faults. We are called to be
completely honest with the sacred consciousness
which is present in us, and to acknowledge our
failings with humble hearts, so that we may
experience forgiveness, both by granting
forgiveness to others and by accepting the gifts of
the Infinite Process expressed in our life.

Fountain of all relationship, you are our
relationships themselves and the unlimited basis
of all; help us to recall the teachings of your

prophets and saints that by means of true humility our lives may always be refreshed and restored. And in order that we might begin life anew, co-creators with you of every moment of our lives, we offer this acknowledgement:

- ◆ We recognize that in our blindness we have lived self-centered lives,
- ◆ We reflect on the actions that we should have taken but did not take.

[Silence]

- ◆ And we consider the acts that we have performed that we should not have.

[Silence]

- ◆ We have been estranged from you, heavenly Spirit,
  Although you appear to us in the love of friends and family.

- ◆ To heal that breach,
  Let us envision ourselves as the compassionate people that we could be,
  Whose every action is an expression of the Christ within.

- We commit to right those wrongs we have
  committed,
  To the extent they can be corrected,
- And we forgive ourselves of those wrongs
  that cannot be remedied,
  Not in selfishness, but to free ourselves to
  become the people we can be.

- To everyone who has wronged us, we forgive
  and forget their faults,
- We put aside our injuries and any desire for
  redress.
- We accept unconditional forgiveness, and
  we give it.

The Words of Assurance
For no one has ever seen God,
But if we love one another God lives in us.
For God is love,
And those who abide in love abide in God.

1 JOHN 12, 16

**The Prayers of Thanksgiving
for Forgiveness**
Holy Presence,
You offer us

The continual power of renewal,
The ability to be restored.

We seek a new beginning by releasing our fear,
Abandoning concern for self,
And placing our trust in your Spirit,
So that in this life, and at the last,
We may share in your timeless joy:
Free from sorrow, regret, and fear,
Living the message of the Christ within,
That all of reality is God's relationship with God.

The Words of Assurance
I will lift the stone from your heart,
And a new spirit I will put within you.
                                        EZEKIEL 36:26

The Response
For this is to live the life eternal:
To experience our indivisible relationship with
     God.
                                        JOHN 17:3

The Lesson
God is spirit,
And those who worship

Must worship in spirit and in truth.

JOHN 4:24

The Assurance

I am Present.

EXODUS 3:14

Canticle

The Boundless is our home and strength,
Therefore we will not fear.
Though the earth be moved,
Though the mountains are carried into the midst
    of the sea.
God is a river in which every stream is joined,
God is in our midst and shall not be moved.
People rage, their kingdoms are destroyed,
But when we open ourselves to the Divine Unity,
All that is earthly melts away.
Come behold the works of the Immeasurable,
Then our conflicts shall cease, and our weapons
    will be broken.
Be still and know that I am God.

PSALM 46

[Silence]

Te Deum
Refreshed, cleansed, renewed,
We resolve to begin again.

We swim in a sea of God,
We lift up our hearts,

We lift them up to you,
The Ever Present
Living Reality.

THANKSGIVINGS
Choose one or more of the following thanksgivings:

Thanksgiving for Plenty
Source of nature and of all relationships, you are
our food and drink, the air we breathe, the space
we inhabit, the time we live. Grantor of life, you
provided us with this world and are present in it.
We give thanks for the clothing we wear, the food
we consume, the friendship and love we
experience, and for our possessions, to which we
are too greatly attached. By your grace allow us to

be satisfied with what we have, and save us from
wanting that which we do not possess, through
your goodness and mercy.
Amen.

Thanksgiving for Friends and Family

Spirit of companionship and caring, we express
our heartfelt gratitude for the company of our
friends and family, through whom we experience
your gift of love. Help us to burst the bonds of
self-concern, and to extend to all those with whom
we come in contact the priceless riches of
compassion and empathy, so that in our time we
may truly experience the heaven on earth that you
have offered to us, through the power of the Christ
within us.

Amen.

Thanksgiving for Freedom

Eternal provider of freedom and order, who
responds to our world and experiences it with us,
we give thanks for the gift of freedom of thought
and movement, and we pray that in the exercise of

these wonderful gifts we may act in gladness of
heart, and in ways that are consistent with your
commandments, and move closer to the
experience of your heavenly kingdom, through
your Holy Spirit.
Amen.

Thanksgiving for Doubt
Source of awareness and thought, we give thanks
for your creating in us the ability to question,
through which we have discovered that every
aspect of your creation, however large or small, is
unlimited. We give thanks for the ability to
perceive this world from many points of view, and
for the capacity to sense, through the activity of
our minds, your own inexhaustible nature.
Amen.

Thanksgiving for Beauty
Holy Unity, we give thanks to you for the deep
blue of the sky, the violin's music, the green of the
forest, the enveloping fog, the reflection of clouds
on still water, the morning dew, the mockingbird's

song, the shade of trees, and the warmth of the
sun. We see and hear you in all these experiences
and more, and for them we give thanks.
Amen.

General Thanksgiving
Everlasting and continuous source of affection, we
thank you for all the blessings of this life. And
particularly we give thanks for ————.

Help us to give rebirth to the Christ within, by
thankful and compassionate living, so that we
may serve your Spirit not only with our words,
but also in our acts, by extending goodness and
mercy to all our neighbors. This we pray in the
spirit of Christ, to whom, with you and the Holy
Spirit moving in the world at this and every
moment in time, be all honor and glory, in this
world without end.
Amen.

The Lord's Prayer
Unfathomable God, ground of our being,
We hallow the names we give you.
Open our hearts to your kingdom,

Teach us to be thankful for our daily bread.
Help us to learn that we live in forgiveness to the
    extent that we forgive,
And deliver us from self-centered existence.
For only by living in compassion and freedom
    from selfishness
May we experience your kingdom, your power,
    and your glory.
Amen.

Closing Sentences
Jesus said:
The kingdom of God is not found by
    observation:
We cannot say look here, or look there!
For the kingdom of God is within you.
                    LUKE 17:20–21

The Benediction
We believe that the sleeping Christ lies always in
    our hearts,
Ready to rise from the dead in every act of
    loving-kindness.
We trust that if we have true humility,

Which is the courage to abandon self-concern
    and fear,
The spirit of Christ will awaken in us,
And through it we will experience
The joy of self-transcendence,
And the peace that passes all understanding.

The Concluding Prayer of the Church

Everlasting Beyond at the center of our being,
whose universe is a daily miracle, send to all
people the carefree atmosphere of your grace, the
continual dew of your blessings; endow us with
the sense of your presence, bestow on us true
happiness, and bring us into your timeless
kingdom by awakening the Christ within our
hearts, the Holy Spirit of compassion and joy.
Amen.

A SERVICE OF EVENING PRAYER

The Invocation

Mystery of mysteries,
You act in this world from another dimension.
Each moment you bring all of creation into
    being,
Again and again we receive your gifts.
Mysterious Beyond at the center of all,
Whose universe is a never-ending miracle,
Endow us now, at the end of this day
With the sense of your presence.
Bestow on us peace as we prepare to rest,
And bring us into the awareness
That we are part of your timeless kingdom,
Now and forever.
Amen.

The Greeting

Great is our God above all gods.
For who is able to comprehend God,
Since the heaven and heaven of heavens
Cannot contain the mystery of our being?

2 CHRONICLES 2:5–6

The Words of Assurance

I came forth from beyond this world,
And I covered the earth like a mist.
I had my tent in the heights,
And my throne in the clouds.
Over the sea and the earth I searched for rest,
And looked to see where I might pitch my tent.
Then I pitched my tent in humankind.
Now I am like a vine putting out graceful shoots,
Approach me and take your fill of my fruits.
They who eat of me will hunger no more,
Whoever drinks of me will thirst no more.
From eternity I came,
And for eternity I will remain.

ECCLESIASTICUS 24

Prayers of Petition

Choose one of the following options:

Infinite Unity,

You surround us,
You permeate us.
Everywhere we look,
There you are.
We swim in a sea that is made of you.
Lift every concern from our hearts,
Fill us with your being,
Awake us to the knowledge
That we rest in you,
Now and forever.
Amen.

Holy and Immortal One,
Remind us of our mortality
So that we may enter fully into the present.
Ground us in the reality of your eternal now,
So that we may completely live each moment.
Allow your divinity to penetrate us,
And teach us to rest in you;
Not as a fleeting experience,
But as a way of being.
As sleep takes us into another dimension
Assist us to trust completely in your eternal
    unfolding.
Amen.

A Prayer of Thanksgiving

Incomprehensible Creator,
If we could conceive of all the worlds that exist,
The stars in their courses,
The galaxies without number,
They would be less than your kingdom within us:
The place of freedom from place,
The time of freedom from time.
As this day ends, we thank you for allowing us
The priceless gift of experiencing this marvelous
    world.
May the thanks we express with our lips
Reflect the thanks we feel in our hearts.
Amen.

A Confession of Faith

Unwavering Presence,
We came from you,
We live in you,
We will die in you.
You are every thought we have,
And every experience.
You rest behind our eyes
And in the clouds before us.

You are the night sky,
The waves on the dark waters,
And the medium in which they move.
You are the source of our consciousness
And consciousness itself.
You are the love of friends and family,
You are the mystery of relationship.
Throughout this day you preserved us
For a purpose we need not understand.
Assist us to see you in all,
And to be worthy of our inheritance.
Amen.

Thanksgiving for This Day

Divine Unifier of all that exists,
Through our thoughts and actions during this
    irreplaceable day,
We have contributed to the process of your
    world, which we co-create with you.
As we end this day,
We give sincere thanks for all that we have
    received this day.
We forgive those who have wronged us.
And because we pledge that tomorrow we will be

better persons than we were today,
We forgive ourselves of the wrongs we have done.

A Prayer of Blessing

Living center of our being,
Through the message of Jesus
And the teachings of those who have come
    before us,
We have learned that transformed existence is
    always possible
For all those who sincerely attempt to live lives of
    loving-kindness
And who accept forgiveness for past failures.
As this day ends we seek
Not the false happiness of this world,
But the authentic peace of the blessed,
The comfort of remembering that we are,
Always and everywhere,
In union with you
Inexhaustible River of Life.
Amen.

Words of Assurance for Eventide

We dwell in the shelter of the Most High,
The Infinite Unity of all

Is our home.
We will not fear any terror of this night
Nor of any sickness that stalks the darkness.
We have made the Unlimited our refuge,
The Boundless our habitation.
Because God is bound to us in love,
With full life and complete trust will we live.

PSALM 91

The Concluding Prayer of the Church

Eternal Presence,
You offer us
The continual power of renewal,
The ability to be restored.
Therefore, as we prepare for rest,
We let go of every fear,
We abandon concern for self,
And we place our trust in your spirit.
So that as we end this day,
And at the last,
We may share in your timeless joy:
Free from sorrow, regret, and fear,
Resting in the knowledge
That you pervade all of reality.
Amen.

The Benediction
Endless Grace,
Tonight, as we shed the events of the day,
We seek to free ourselves of everything that
    blocks us from you.
Empty of every want,
Empty of every need,
Empty of desire to be anything but what we are,
Here in this moment of the eternal Now,
Efficiency and purpose are set aside.
We do not have,
We do not strive,
We are.
And we rest in you.
Amen.

A MEMORIAL SERVICE IN THANKSGIVING FOR THE LIFE OF ONE DEPARTED

Now outside the world of deeds, our *sister* has been called. We live on, soon to join *her*, swept onward by your inexorable tide toward that state where all are free of time and space, joined with you in life and at the last, forever a part of the endless, loving, incomprehensible Beyond in the midst of all.

Eternal Encompasser, for the life of our *sister*, we give you thanks. We remember *her* with love and confidence. We do not fear for *her* or for ourselves, for you are with *her*, and *she* is with you.

Words of Assurance

For we are sure that neither death, nor life, nor angels, nor principalities, not things present, nor things to come, nor powers, nor height, nor

depth, nor anything else in all creation, can
separate us from the love of God.

ROMANS 8:38–39

If we live, we live in God,
And if we die, we die in God.
Therefore, whether we live or whether we die,
We are God's.

ROMANS 14:7–8

Though we speak much we cannot reach the end,
And the sum of all our words is:
God is All,
And God is greater than creation.

SIRACH 43:27–28

As the heavens are higher than the earth,
So are my ways higher than your ways,
And my thoughts higher than your thoughts.

ISAIAH 55:9

We brought nothing into this world, and we can
carry nothing out.
The Creator gave and has taken away.

Blessed be the Creator and creation.

1 TIMOTHY 6:7; JOB 1:21

Readings from the Psalms

Mystery of mysteries,
You have been our dwelling place for all
    generations.
Before the mountains were brought forth,
Before the world was formed,
From everlasting to everlasting,
You are.
You bring us into life
And return us to dust.
A thousand years in your sight
Are as a watch in the night.
You sweep us away,
Like grass that is green in the morning,
And in the evening is cut down and withers.
For our days pass away,
And our years come to an end like a sigh.
The days of our years are threescore years
    and ten,
And if by reason of strength they be fourscore years,
They are soon cut off, and we fly away.

So teach us to number our days that we may
   apply our hearts to wisdom.
Make us glad in the morning and the evening of
   our days,
Let the beauty of your presence be revealed to us
   and to our children.
Let us be satisfied with your gifts,
That we may rejoice and be glad in all our days.
Let your work appear through us,
And our children's children.
Let the beauty of the Divine be in us,
And the works of our hands establish it.
From eternity to eternity, you are our God.

PSALM 90

Where shall we go from your spirit?
Or where shall we flee from your presence?
If we ascend up into heaven,
You are there:
If we make our bed in hell,
You are there.
If we take the wings of the morning,
And dwell in the uttermost parts of the sky,
Even there your hands shall hold us.

If we say, surely the darkness shall cover us,
Even the night shall be light.
For the darkness does not hide from you,
But the night shines as the day,
The darkness and the light are both alike to you.
For you have possessed us always;
You encompassed us in our mothers' wombs.

PSALM 139:7–13

A Statement of Faith

The whole of reality is God relating to God,
We are to God as a wave is to the sea.
God is the thinker and the thought,
The Creator and the Created,
The force of gravity,
The wind on the waters,
The air we breathe,
The water we drink,
The bread we eat,
The process of life and death.

Acting in all that is,
Evolving and changing,
Uncreated, ultimate, unfathomable,

From whom all things proceed,
Of which all things are,
To which all things return.

God is the universe that has no edge,
The morning dew and the center of the sun,
God is between us,
God is beyond us,
God is breathing us.
Rising, increasing, changing,
The great miracle and enigma,
Outside all categories,
The relationship of all relationships,
The medium of all communication,
The cause of love and love itself.
God in ourselves, our souls and bodies.

God is the present moment,
The Now that never ceases to be,
Infinite in all directions.

God fills the universe.
We are, always and everywhere,
Aspects of the eternal unity.

For if we could conceive all the worlds that exist,
They would be less than God's kingdom within
    us,
The place of freedom from place,
The time of freedom from time.

Words of Comfort

Am I not a God at hand, and not a God afar off?
Can any hide in secret places that I shall not
    perceive?
Do not I fill heaven and earth?

JEREMIAH 23:24

"I am the Alpha and the Omega, the beginning
    and the end."

REVELATION 21:6

The Eternal is neither timelessness, nor is it
    endless time.
We speak in metaphors taken from time,
But the metaphors are only metaphors,
Not Reality itself.
In life we move toward a state that is not yet,
Incessantly we leave behind a state that is no more.

Yet past and future only exist as a part of the
    present,
And the present is a deep mystery.
It is gone the instant we try to hold it,
Yet it is always with us.
Each moment in time is part of the Eternal,
The Eternal that provides us with time and
    transcends it.
We seem to be bound up in time,
But we live and die in the source of time,
The deepest mystery of all:
The living and eternal God.

Concluding Words

In the midst of life we are in death. Of whom can
we seek comfort but from you, the secret of our
hearts. Reassure us, eternal Presence, in our last
hour, lest we forget that we always have been, and
always will be, in your embrace.

For as much as it is the nature of the
everlasting Reality that we live and then die, our
sister has been returned to the living Source of
the universe. At birth, *she* came from God; during
life, *she* was a manifestation of God; in death, *she*

is in God. From where *she* came, there *she* has returned, from the Infinite to the Infinite. Thanks be to God for *her* and for the Eternal Spirit who acted in *her*.

A SERVICE OF COMMEMORATION FOR OUR UNION

Opening Sentences

As the deer longs for the water brook, so long our
souls for you, O God.

We thirst for God, for the living God.

PSALM 42:1–2

The Assurance

"Bidden or not bidden, God is present."[11]

Invocation

Unbroken Wholeness,

Help us to open our hearts to you and to all
beings.

Dispel the illusion of separation.

Teach us to perceive your presence.

Through our actions and our thoughts,

We carry out the work of eternity.

Assist us to make this world a world of compassion.
Awake the Spirit of Christ in us,
And thereby grant us the power of fearless
    existence.
Amen.

A Confession of Faith
We have faith that the whole of reality is God
    relating to God,
That we are to God as a wave is to the sea.
God is the thinker and the thought,
The force of gravity,
The wind on the waters,
The process of change,
The air we breathe,
The water we drink,
The bread we eat.

God is the nameless origin of names,
Acting in all that is,
Evolving and changing,
Uncreated, ultimate, unfathomable,
From whom all things proceed,
Of which all things are,

To which all things return.

God is the universe that has no edge,
The morning dew and the center of the sun,
God between us,
God beyond us,
God breathing us.
Rising, increasing, changing,
The great miracle and enigma,
Outside all categories,
The relationship of all relationships,
The medium of all communication,
The cause of love and love itself,
God in ourselves, our souls and bodies.

God is the source of time and endless time itself.
God is the present moment,
The ungraspable Now that never ceases to be,
Infinite in all directions.

God fills the universe.
We are, always and everywhere,
Aspects of eternal unity.
If we could conceive all the worlds that exist,

They would be less than God's kingdom within
    us,
The place of freedom from place,
The time of freedom from time.

A Reading from Scripture
Lay not up for yourselves treasure upon the earth,
Where moth and rot corrupt, and where thieves
    break through and steal:
But lay up for yourselves heavenly treasures,
Where neither rust nor moth corrupt,
And where thieves do not break through and
    steal.

MATTHEW 6:19–21

A Reading
Our true nature is that we are one with the
    eternal Source,
When we were created, we were created by God,
While we live, we live in God,
When we die, we die in God.
Yet foolishly we grant to "things" an importance
    they do not have.
We are blind to the unity of the world.

We conceal God from ourselves.
We swim in the sea of God,
But we do not sense the living water that
    surrounds us.
We lack the compassion that would reveal our
    kinship,
That would dispel every fear,
And bring genuine peace and joy.

A Prayer

We have been estranged from you, Divine Spirit,
ground of our existence, the creative energy of all
that is. You are the harmony that makes us
possible, who appears to us in the love of friends
and family, the kindness of strangers, and the
workings of the world. All this, and more, is you,
the God who gave us love. Teach us, and we will
listen.
Amen.

The Summary of the Law

Choose one or more of these options:

Whatever you would that others would do to you,
So do to them, for this is the law and the prophets.

                    MATTHEW 7:12

You shall not want anything that is not yours.
EXODUS 20:17

You shall love the Holy Mystery
Unfolding in creation,
The Eternal Miracle,
The Living Web of Existence,
With all your heart,
With all your soul,
With all your mind,
And with all your strength.
This is the first and greatest commandment.
And the second is the same:
You shall love your neighbor as yourself.
On these two commandments
Hang all the law and the prophets.
MATTHEW 22:37–40

Love your enemies, do good to those who hate
you, bless those who curse you, pray for those
who mistreat you, and you will be the children of
God. Be compassionate. Do not judge and you
will not be judged, give and you will be given
gifts, forgive and you will receive forgiveness. For

you are made in God's image as a co-creator of
your world, and thus the amount you measure
out is the measure you will obtain.

LUKE 6:27, 35–38

Be not deceived, God is not mocked: for
whatsoever we sow, so shall we reap.

GALATIANS 6:7

If you do away with the desire to use others,
With the clenched fist, the wicked word,
If you give your bread to the hungry,
And relief to the oppressed,
If you free yourself from the delusion of
    separateness,
Your light shall shine in the darkness,
And your shadow shall be as noon.
God will always be with you,
And you will have relief in the desert places.
You will be like a spring
Whose waters never run dry.

ISAIAH 58:7–12

Anyone who fails to love cannot know God, for
    God is love.

No one has ever seen God, but when we love one
    another, God lives in us.

1 JOHN 4:8, 12

The Confession of Sin

We have been estranged from you, Divine Spirit,
ground of our existence, the creative energy of all
that is. You are the Unity who makes us possible,
who appears to us in the love of friends and
family, in the kindness of strangers, and in the
workings of the world. All this, and more, is you,
the God who gave us love.

We examine our lives in the light of your
commandment to reject all idols, especially the
false gods of security, acclaim, and power.

We seek to dispel the myth of separation, and to
see you in all things and in all our actions, and to
place you at the center of our lives.

And to that end, we now confront our failings
and wrongdoings honestly and with complete
candor.

- We have been selfish.
- We have lacked compassion.
- We have been ungrateful for what we have.
- We have spent time foolishly, forgetting that it is irreplaceable.
- And we have not been as happy as we were made to be.

Recognizing that through our thoughts and actions we contribute to the development of your world, which we co-create with you, we each ask ourselves:

- What have I given?
- What have I received?
- What harm have I done?
- What joy have I spread?

[Silence]

We are aware that if we fail to act now, in the never-ending present, we cannot experience that heavenly state of full, fearless, and joyful life that is our rightful birthright as your hands and eyes, Holy and Eternal Spirit.

Therefore, having examined our actions and our thoughts, we solemnly vow:

- If we have injured our neighbor we shall, to the full extent of our power to do so, admit our fault to him or her, and make restitution.
- If wrong has been done to us, we forgive that wrong, just as we wish to be forgiven ourselves.
- And if we cannot quiet our consciences alone, we will seek a trusted counselor and confess our failings, so to receive wisdom and advice and make a new beginning.

The Words of Promise
I will lift the stone from your heart,
And a new spirit I will put within you.
                                    EZEKIEL 36:26

The Prayers for Forgiveness
Living Center of our being, through the message of Jesus and the teachings of those who have come before us, we have learned that

transformed, bold, and joyful existence is always
available to those who live lives of loving-
kindness, who accept forgiveness for past failures,
and who sincerely intend to lead a new life.

Give us the courage to accept forgiveness now,
Not as an abstract assertion,
But as an essential encounter with your creative
    power.

We seek
Not the false happiness of this world,
But the authentic joy and glory of the blessed,
Which consists in the enjoyment of the whole
    world
In spiritual union with God.

We accept forgiveness and we give it, sincerely
    promising to lead a new life following your
    commandments.

The Assurance
Be renewed in spirit and in mind.

EPHESIANS 4:23

A Meditation

We believe that the sleeping Christ lies always in
    our hearts,
Ready to rise from the dead in every act of
    loving-kindness.
We believe that if we have true humility,
Which is the courage to abandon self-concern
    and fear,
The Spirit of Christ will awaken in us,
And through it we will experience
The joy of self-transcendence,
And the peace that passes all understanding.

We seek to be truly thankful for the joys of
    existence, and to trust in your grace;
    therefore, without reservation,
We discard the cares of the world, and
    gratefully and joyfully accept the
    overwhelming gift of life.

The Comfortable Words

Be still and know that I am God.
                                    PSALM 46:10

The Words of Union

Here in this moment of the eternal Now,
Efficiency and purpose are set aside.
We let go of self-concern,
We quiet our hearts and minds,
We experience the eternal Presence,
We join in the mystery of our union with
     Eternity.
We do not *have.*
We do not *strive.*
We *are,*
And God and we are one.

[Silence]

Response

For this is to live the life eternal:
To experience our indivisible relationship with
God.

JOHN 17:3

God answered Moses and said: "I am Present."

EXODUS 3:14

The Holy Presence is always with us.
It is not found, because it is always here.

It is the unwavering, the constant embrace.
It is not a state of being or a state of mind,
It is the state in which all states come and go.
There are no words to describe the Presence.
It is the words, the sky we breathe,
The world we see,
The eyes through which we see,
And the awareness behind our eyes.

Psalm
Eternal Providence is my light and my salvation:
Whom shall I fear?
The spirit within is the strength of my life:
Of whom shall I be afraid?
Though a host should encamp against me,
My heart shall not tremble.
Though war should rise up in opposition to me,
In the embrace of the Boundless will I be
    confident.
When my father and mother forsake me,
    God supports me.
In the midst of my enemies the Unlimited
    envelops me.
I rest in the grace of the Everlasting.

PSALM 27

Closing Sentences

Choose one or more of these options:
Be renewed in spirit and mind.

EPHESIANS 4:23

For in you we live, and move, and have our being.

ACTS 17:28

We lift up our hearts,
We lift them up unto the Living Presence,
The Christ within,
The timeless and divine One,
In whom we live and move and have our being.

In your presence is fullness of joy.

PSALM 16:11

Rejoice in the Encompassing Always, and again I say, rejoice.

PHILIPPIANS 4:4

The Prayers of Benediction

Renewed and refreshed, we begin again, offering ourselves, our souls, and bodies, heirs through hope of your timeless kingdom; members incorporate in the mystical body of Christ.

In life we are in grace. In every moment and in every place, we live suspended in the web of Divinity of which we are made. Therefore, we leave our fears and concerns behind, and place our complete trust in the Infinite. We rest in the never-ending Presence. We merge our spirits with the Holy Spirit and with one another in mystical delight in our world. We call forth from within ourselves the spirit of the Christ within, of forgiveness and unconditional compassion, resurrected and incarnate in this place and time; we offer Christ's kindness to one another.

Eternal Source, so assist us by your grace that we may continue in this holy fellowship, and do all the good works we are capable of doing. Through the spirit of Christ, help us to act in unselfish care for one another and for all your creation, in this world without end.

We, who are capable of being so many different selves, commit to a radical trust in Divine Providence. We vow to be couriers of all that is holy in this world.
Amen.

NOTES

1. Martin Buber, *The Way of Response,* ed. N. N. Glatzer (New York: Schocken Books, 1971), pp. 38–39.

2. Werner Heisenberg, winner of the Nobel Prize for his work in physics, quoted in *Quantum Questions,* ed. Ken Wilbur (Boulder, Colo.: New Science Library, 1984), p. 44.

3. Dietrich Bonhoeffer, *Letters and Papers From Prison,* 3rd ed. (New York: Macmillan, 1967).

4. For this phrase I thank Stephen L. Carter, the author of *The Culture of Disbelief: How American Law and Politics Trivialize Religious Devotion* (London: Anchor, 1994). According to *The Wall Street Journal,* 11 September 2000, P1, the percentage of American regular churchgoers is about 20 percent.

5. I use the word "convergence" deliberately, to suggest areas of consistency. But it would be incorrect to say that these brilliant and divergent men and women (see the bibliography for some of their works) all agree with one another, or with the conclusions I have expressed.

6. Annie Dillard, quoting University of Chicago theologian David Tracy, in "Holy Sparks: A Prayer for the Silent God," *Notre Dame Magazine,* Winter 1998–99.

7. Some of the noted theologians whose views are either panentheist or closely similar to panentheism are: Nicolas

Berdyaev (Eastern Orthodox), Marcus Borg (Protestant), Martin Buber (Jewish), Teilhard de Chardin (Catholic), John B. Cobb Jr. (Protestant), David A. Cooper (Jewish), Ecknath Easwaren (Hindu), Matthew Fox (Protestant, former Catholic), David Ray Griffin (Protestant), Allama Muhammad Iqbal (Muslim), H. Richard Niebuhr (Protestant), Daniel C. Matt (Jewish), Sallie McFague (Protestant), Thomas Merton (Catholic), Seyyed Hossin Nasr (Muslim), Schubert Ogden (Protestant), Raimundo Panikkar (Catholic), Norman Pittenger (Protestant), Sarvepalli Radhakrishnan (Hindu), J. A. T. Robinson (Protestant), Albert Schweitzer (Protestant), Marjorie Suchochi (Protestant), John Shelby Spong (Protestant), Paul Tillich (Protestant), David Tracy (Protestant), Evelyn Underhill (Protestant), Alan Watts (Protestant), Henry Wieman (Unitarian), and Daniel Day Williams (Protestant).

Philosophers who can be said to be panentheists include: Henri Louis Bergson, Gustav Fechner, Lewis S. Ford, Charles Hartshorne, C. S. Pierce, Otto Pfleiderer, Joseph Schelling, Bernadino Varisco, Donald Viney, Paul Weiss, and Alfred North Whitehead.

The writings of virtually every mystic, regardless of religion, from Saint Teresa to Rumi, articulate the central principles of panentheist thought: mystery, unity, and the presence of the divine. Thus, the following description of the mystic character in the opening sentences of Ursula King's history of Christian mystics: "A mystic is a person who is deeply aware of the powerful presence of the divine Spirit: someone who seeks, above all, the knowledge and love of

God and who experiences to an extraordinary degree the profoundly personal encounter with the energy of divine life. Mystics often perceive the presence of God throughout the world of nature and in all that is alive, leading to the transfiguration of all that is around them." Ursula King, *Christian Mystics: Their Lives & Legacies Throughout the Ages* (Mahwah, N.J.: Hidden Spring, 2001).

Many poets have expressed such a viewpoint, including: William Blake, John Donne, Elizabeth Barrett Browning, T. S. Elliot, Mary Oliver, George Herbert, Emily Dickinson, Henry Vaughan, Edna St. Vincent Milay, Thomas Traherne, Denise Levertov, and William Wordsworth.

8. Saint Augustine, *Homily on Psalm 99.6,* cited in Kenneth Leech, *Experiencing God: Theology as Spirituality* (New York: Harper & Row, 1985), p. 324.

9. The references to the Bible are not meant to indicate that the verse has been quoted, but to direct the reader to the source of the restatement.

10. Thomas Traherne, *Centuries, I.29,* quoted in Graham Dowell, *Enjoying the World: The Rediscovery of Thomas Traherne* (Harrisburg, Pa.: Morehouse Publishing, 1990), p. 12.

11. "These words were carved in Latin over [Carl] Jung's front door…. They are also on Jung's tombstone." In Marcus J. Borg, *The God We Never Knew* (New York: HarperCollins, 1998), p. 49.

BIBLIOGRAPHY

Barrow, John D. *The World Within the World*. Oxford:
Oxford University Press, 1988.

von Bertalanffy, Ludwig. *Modern Theories of Development:
An Introduction to Theoretical Biology*. Translated by J.
H. Woodger. New York: Harper, 1960.

Bonhoeffer, Dietrich. *Letters and Papers From from Prison*.
3rd ed. New York: Macmillan, 1967.

Bohm, David. *On Creativity*. London: Routledge, 1998.

————. *Wholeness and the Implicate Order*. London:
Routledge & Kegan Paul, 1980.

Borg, Marcus J. *The God We Never Knew*. New York: Harper
Collins, 1998.

Borg, Marcus J., ed. *God At 2000*. Harrisburg, Pa.:
Morehouse Publishing, 2001.

Borg, Marcus J. and N. T. Wright, *The Meaning of Jesus:
Two Visions*. San Francisco: Harper Collins, 1998.

Buber, Martin. *Tales of the Hasidim*. New York: Schocken
Books, 1947.

———— *The Way of Response*, ed. N. N. Glatzer. New York:
Schocken Books, 1971.

Carrigan, Henry L., Jr., ed. *The Way of Perfection by Saint Teresa of Avila.* Brewster, Mass.: Paraclete Press, 2000.

Cobb, John B. *Charles Hartshorne: The Einstein of Religious Thought, 1897–2000.* Claremont, Calif.: The Center for Process Studies, 2001.

Cousins, Norman. Commentator,. *Nobel Prize Conversations.* Dallas, Tex.: Saybrook Publishing Company, 1985.

Clayton, P. *God and Contemporary Science.* Edinburgh: Edinburgh University Press, 1997.

de Chardin, Teilhard. *The Divine Milieu.* New York: Harper & Row, 1960.

———. *The Heart of the Matter.* New York: Harcourt Brace Jovanovich, 1976.

Cooper, David A. *God Is a Verb: Kabala and the Practice of Mystical Judaism.* New York: Riverhead Books / Penguin, 1997.

Dennett, Daniel. *Consciousness Explained.* Boston: MIT Press, 1991.

Dillard, Annie. *For the Time Being.* New York: Alfred A. Knopf, 1999.

Dombrowski, Daniel. "Wordsworth's Panentheism." *Wordsworth Circle* 16 (1985).

Dowell, Graham. *Enjoying the World: The Rediscovery of Thomas Traherne.* Harrisburg, Pa.: Morehouse Publishing, 1990.

Dyson, Freeman. *Infinite In All Directions.* Gifford Lectures. New York: Harper & Row, 1988.

Easwaren, Ecknath, translator. *The Bhagavad-Gita.* New

York: Vintage Books, 1985.

———, trans. *The Dhammapada*. Tomales, Cailf.: Nilgiri Press, 1985.

Farrington, Debra K. *Living Faith Day By Day*. New York: Penguin Putman, 2000.

Feyman, Richard P. *The Pleasure of Finding Things Out*. Cambridge, Mass.: Perseus Publishing, 1999.

Fox, Matthew. *Passion for Creation: The Earth-Honoring Spirituality of Meister Eckhart*. Rochester, Vt.: Inner Traditions, 1991.

James, William. *The Varieties of Religious Experience*. Introduction by Reinhold Niebuhr. New York: Simon & Schuster, 1997.

Matt, C. *The Essential Kabbalah: The Heart of Jewish Mysticism*. Edison, N. J.: Castle Books, 1977.

Hartshorne, Charles and William L. Reese. *Philosophers Speak of God*. Chicago: University of Chicago Press, 1953.

King, Ursula. *Christian Mystics*. Mahwah, N. J.: Paulist Press, 2001.

Kleene, S. C. "The Work of Kurt Godel." *Journal of Symbolic Logic* 41 (1976), and 43 (1978).

Leech, Kenneth. *Experiencing God: Theology as Spirituality*. New York: Harper & Row, 1985.

Malin, Shimon. *Nature Loves to Hide: Quantum Physics and the Nature of Reality, A Western Perspective*. New York: Oxford University Press, 2001.

Margulis, Lynn and Dorian Sagan. *Microcosmos: Four Billion Years from Our Microbial Ancestors*. New York: Simon & Schuster, 1986.

McFague, Sallie. *Models of God*. Philadelphia: Fortress Press, 1987.

Nadeau, Robert and Menos Kafatos. *The Conscious Universe*. New York: Springer Verlag, 2000.

———. *The Non-Local Universe*. New York: Oxford University Press, 1999.

Newberg, Andrew B., Eugene G. DíAquili, and Vince Rause. *Why God Won't Go Away: Brain Science and the Biology of Belief*. New York: Ballantine Books, 2001.

Pandita, Saydaw U. *In This Very Life: The Liberation Teachings of the Buddha*. Somerville, Mass.: Wisdom Publications, 1991.

Panikkar, Raimundo. *The Unknown Christ of Hinduism*. Maryknoll, N.Y.: Orbis Books, 1981.

———. *Invisible Harmony*. Minneapolis: Fortress Press, 1995.

———. *The Vedic Experience*. New Delhi: Motilal Publishers, 1983.

———. *The Silence of God: The Answer of the Buddha*. Maryknoll, N.Y.: Orbis Books, 1989.

Peacocke, A. R. *Creation and the World of Science*. Oxford: Oxford University Press, 1979.

Prigogine, Ilya and Yves Elskens. "Irreversibility, Scholasticity and Non-locality in Classical Dynamics. In Quantum Implications, ed. Basil J. Hiley and F. David Peat. London: Routledge & Keegan Paul, 1987.

Sanford, John A. *The Kingdom Within*. New York: Paulist Press, 1970.

Stapp, Henry P. *Mind, Matter, and Quantum Mechanics*.

Heidelberg: Springer Verlag, 1993.

Tickle, Phyllis, ed. *The Divine Hours*. 4 vols. New York: Doubleday, 2001.

Tillich, Paul. *The Dynamics of Faith*. New York: Harper & Row, 1957.

———. *The Essential Tillich*. Edited by E. Forrester Church. New York: Collier, 1987.

———. *The Eternal Now*. New York: Charles Scribner's Sons, 1963.

———. "Religious Symbols and Our Knowledge." *Christian Scholar*, September 1955. Copyright 1955 by *Soundings* magazine.

Lao Tzu. *Tao Te Ching*. Edited by Paul K. T. Sih. New York: St. John's University Press, 1961.

Underhill, Evelyn. *Mysticism: A Study in the Nature and Development of Man's Spiritual Consciousness*. New York: World, 1911.

Watson, Burton. *The Complete Works of Chang Tzu*. New York: Columbia University Press, 1968.

Watts, Alan. *Behold the Spirit*. New York: Random House, 1947.

Weiss, Paul. "The Living System." In *Beyond Reductionism: New Perspectives in the Life Sciences*, ed. A. Koestler and J. R. Smythies. Boston: Beacon, 1964.

Wilbur, Ken, ed. *Quantum Questions*. Boulder, Colo.: New Science Library, 1984.

Wittgenstein, Ludwig. *Tractatus Logico-Philosophicus*. London: Routledge, 1981.